In celebration of

_____

_____

_____

_____

_____

Guests

Guests

_____   _____

_____   _____

_____   _____

_____   _____

_____   _____

_____   _____

_____   _____

_____   _____

_____   _____

_____   _____

_____   _____

_____   _____

_____   _____

_____   _____

_____   _____

_____   _____

Guests

Guests

Guests

Message/Wishes

Name:

Message/Wishes

Name:

Message/Wishes

Name:

Message/Wishes

Name:

Message/Wishes

Name:

Message/Wishes

Name:

Message/Wishes

Name:

Message/Wishes

Name:

Message/Wishes

Name:

Message/Wishes

Name:

Message/Wishes

Name:

Message/Wishes

Name:

Message/Wishes

Name:

Message/Wishes

Name:

Message/Wishes

Name:

Message/Wishes

Name:

Message/Wishes

Name:

Message/Wishes

Name:

Message/Wishes

Name:

Message/Wishes

Name:

Message/Wishes

Name:

Message/Wishes

Name:

Message/Wishes

Name:

Message/Wishes

Name:

Message/Wishes

Name:

Message/Wishes

Name:

Message/Wishes

Name:

Message/Wishes

Name:

Message/Wishes

Name:

Message/Wishes

Name:

Message/Wishes

Name:

Message/Wishes

Name:

Message/Wishes

Name:

Message/Wishes

Name:

Message/Wishes

Name:

Message/Wishes

Name:

Message/Wishes

Name:

Message/Wishes

Name:

Message/Wishes

Name:

Message/Wishes

Name:

Message/Wishes

Name:

Message/Wishes

Name:

Message/Wishes

Name:

Message/Wishes

Name:

Message/Wishes
Name:

Message/Wishes
Name:

Message/Wishes
Name:

Message/Wishes
Name:

Message/Wishes

Name:

Message/Wishes

Name:

Message/Wishes

Name:

Message/Wishes

Name:

Message/Wishes

Name:

Message/Wishes

Name:

Message/Wishes

Name:

Message/Wishes

Name:

Message/Wishes

Name:

Message/Wishes

Name:

Message/Wishes

Name:

Message/Wishes

Name:

Message/Wishes

Name:

Message/Wishes

Name:

Message/Wishes

Name:

Message/Wishes

Name:

Message/Wishes

Name:

Message/Wishes

Name:

Message/Wishes

Name:

Message/Wishes

Name:

Message/Wishes

Name:

Message/Wishes

Name:

Message/Wishes

Name:

Message/Wishes

Name:

Message/Wishes

Name:

Message/Wishes

Name:

Message/Wishes

Name:

Message/Wishes

Name:

Message/Wishes

Name:

Message/Wishes

Name:

Message/Wishes

Name:

Message/Wishes

Name:

Message/Wishes

Name:

Message/Wishes

Name:

Message/Wishes

Name:

Message/Wishes

Name:

Message/Wishes
Name:

Message/Wishes
Name:

Message/Wishes
Name:

Message/Wishes
Name:

Message/Wishes

Name:

Message/Wishes

Name:

Message/Wishes

Name:

Message/Wishes

Name:

Message/Wishes

Name:

Message/Wishes

Name:

Message/Wishes

Name:

Message/Wishes

Name:

Message/Wishes

_____
_____
_____
_____
_____
_____
_____

Name:

Message/Wishes

_____
_____
_____
_____
_____
_____
_____
_____

Name:

Message/Wishes

_____
_____
_____
_____
_____
_____

Name:

Message/Wishes

_____
_____
_____
_____
_____
_____
_____

Name:

Message/Wishes

Name:

Message/Wishes

Name:

Message/Wishes

Name:

Message/Wishes

Name:

Message/Wishes

Name:

Message/Wishes

Name:

Message/Wishes

Name:

Message/Wishes

Name:

Message/Wishes

Name:

Message/Wishes

Name:

Message/Wishes

Name:

Message/Wishes

Name:

Message/Wishes

Name:

Message/Wishes

Name:

Message/Wishes

Name:

Message/Wishes

Name:

Message/Wishes

Name:

Message/Wishes

Name:

Message/Wishes

Name:

Message/Wishes

Name:

Message/Wishes

Name:

Message/Wishes

Name:

Message/Wishes

Name:

Message/Wishes

Name:

Message/Wishes

Name:

Message/Wishes

Name:

Message/Wishes

Name:

Message/Wishes

Name:

Message/Wishes

Name:

Message/Wishes

Name:

Message/Wishes

Name:

Message/Wishes

Name:

Message/Wishes

Name:

Message/Wishes

Name:

Message/Wishes

Name:

Message/Wishes

Name:

Message/Wishes

Name:

Message/Wishes

Name:

Message/Wishes

Name:

Message/Wishes

Name:

Message/Wishes

Name:

Message/Wishes

Name:

Message/Wishes

Name:

Message/Wishes

Name:

Message/Wishes

Name:

Message/Wishes

Name:

Message/Wishes

Name:

Message/Wishes

Name:

Message/Wishes
Name:

Message/Wishes
Name:

Message/Wishes
Name:

Message/Wishes
Name:

Message/Wishes

Name:

Message/Wishes

Name:

Message/Wishes

Name:

Message/Wishes

Name:

Message/Wishes

Name:

Message/Wishes

Name:

Message/Wishes

Name:

Message/Wishes

Name:

Message/Wishes

Name:

Message/Wishes

Name:

Message/Wishes

Name:

Message/Wishes

Name:

Message/Wishes
Name:

Message/Wishes
Name:

Message/Wishes
Name:

Message/Wishes
Name:

Message/Wishes

_____

_____

_____

_____

_____

_____

_____

Name:

Message/Wishes

_____

_____

_____

_____

_____

_____

_____

Name:

Message/Wishes

_____

_____

_____

_____

_____

_____

_____

Name:

Message/Wishes

_____

_____

_____

_____

_____

_____

_____

Name:

Message/Wishes

Name:

Message/Wishes

Name:

Message/Wishes

Name:

Message/Wishes

Name:

Message/Wishes

Name:

Message/Wishes

Name:

Message/Wishes

Name:

Message/Wishes

Name:

Message/Wishes
Name:

Message/Wishes
Name:

Message/Wishes
Name:

Message/Wishes
Name:

Message/Wishes

Name:

Message/Wishes

Name:

Message/Wishes

Name:

Message/Wishes

Name:

Message/Wishes

Name:

Message/Wishes

Name:

Message/Wishes

Name:

Message/Wishes

Name:

Message/Wishes

_____

_____

_____

_____

_____

_____

_____

_____

Name:

Message/Wishes

_____

_____

_____

_____

_____

_____

_____

_____

Name:

Message/Wishes

_____

_____

_____

_____

_____

_____

_____

Name:

Message/Wishes

_____

_____

_____

_____

_____

_____

_____

Name:

Message/Wishes

Name:

Message/Wishes

Name:

Message/Wishes

Name:

Message/Wishes

Name:

Memories

Memories

Memories

Memories

Memories

Memories

Memories

Memories

Memories

Memories

Made in the USA
Coppell, TX
08 May 2024

32085780R00037